EDGE
BOOKS

WAR MACHINES   ATTACK SUBMARINES

The Seawolf Class

by Michael and Gladys Green

Consultant:
Lieutenant Matthew Galan
Public Affairs Officer
Navy Office of Information, New York City

Edge Books are published by Capstone Press
151 Good Counsel Drive, P.O. Box 669, Mankato, Minnesota 56002
www.capstonepress.com

Library of Congress Cataloging-in-Publication Data
Green, Michael, 1952–
     Attack submarines: the Seawolf class / by Michael and Gladys Green.
     p. cm.—(Edge books. War machines)
     Includes bibliographical references and index.
     ISBN 0-7368-2721-8 (hardcover)
     1. Nuclear submarines—United States—Juvenile literature. 2. Seawolf
(Submarine)—Juvenile literature. I. Green, Gladys, 1954– II. Title. III. Edge books.
War machines.
V858.G72 2005
359.9'3834—dc22   2004000756

Summary: Describes the Seawolf class attack submarine, including its history,
equipment, weapons, tactics, and future use with the U.S. Navy.

Editorial Credits
Katy Kudela, editor; Jason Knudson, series designer; Molly Nei, book designer;
     Jo Miller, photo researcher; Eric Kudalis, product planning editor

Photo Credits
DVIC, 16–17; Caroline Kiehner, 7; Jim Brennan, 5, 24
Folio Inc./Y.R. Kaufman, 19
General Dynamics Electric Boat, cover, 9, 27, 28–29
Getty Images Inc./Time Life Pictures/U.S. Navy, 14
U.S. Navy photo, 23; PHC John E. Gay, 11, 12, 20

1 2 3 4 5 6 09 08 07 06 05 04

Table of Contents

CHAPTER 1

The Seawolf in Action

A Seawolf submarine patrols deep below the ocean's surface. It travels far ahead of a U.S. Navy aircraft carrier and other U.S. Navy warships. The Seawolf's crew is on alert. An enemy country has just sent out six attack submarines.

The Seawolf's sonar scans the ocean. The radio waves quickly find the enemy subs. Crew members in the torpedo room load MK-48 torpedoes into launching tubes.

On the captain's command, the crew fires the MK-48s. The MK-48s shoot through the water and destroy the enemy subs.

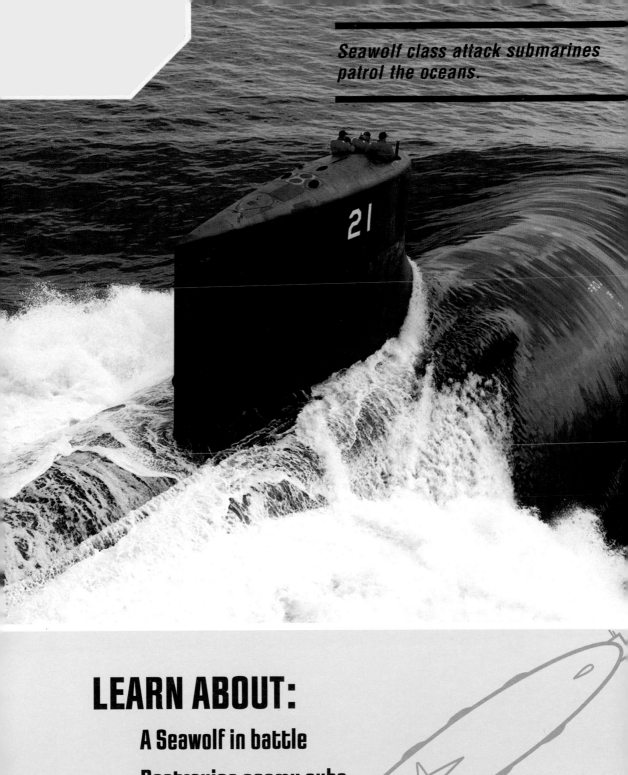

Seawolf class attack submarines patrol the oceans.

LEARN ABOUT:

A Seawolf in battle
Destroying enemy subs
Seawolf history

5

Just before it sinks, an enemy sub sends a radio message to its home base. A U.S. spy satellite picks up the message and sends it to the Seawolf. The Seawolf's crew quickly programs its Tomahawk missiles to hit the enemy base. The crew fires the missiles. A few minutes later, the enemy's base explodes. The U.S. aircraft carrier and its fleet are safe.

Attack Submarines

From 1949 to 1991, the United States and the former Soviet Union had unfriendly relations. Each country feared the other would attack.

The U.S. Navy feared the Soviet Union's powerful submarines. The United States began building attack submarines. The U.S. Navy's largest fleet of attack submarines was the Los Angeles class.

Soon, the Soviet Union built faster submarines. These submarines could dive deeper than the U.S. subs.

In the mid-1980s, the U.S. Navy began building new attack submarines. This class of submarines was designed to move faster and dive deeper than earlier U.S. subs. This class of nuclear-powered submarines was called the Seawolf.

The U.S. Navy planned to build 30 Seawolf class attack submarines. Due to high costs, Congress lowered this number to three.

The USS *Seawolf* entered Navy service in 1997. The following year, the USS *Connecticut* entered Navy service. The USS *Jimmy Carter* is the Navy's third Seawolf class attack submarine.

The USS Connecticut *is a Seawolf class attack sub.*

A Seawolf's hull, or body, is round and smooth. The hull is made of strong metals. These metals can hold up against high water pressure.

The hull has two watertight sections. These sections are the forward and the rear. The forward section contains the control room, weapon systems, and sonar systems. The rear holds the nuclear reactor and propeller. The propeller drives the submarine through the water.

A skinny tower called a sail sits on top of the hull. The sail holds the periscopes and sensors.

Control Room

The control room is inside the hull below the sail. Crew members in the control room operate the sub. The captain and the officer of the deck are in charge of this room.

Crew members can climb to the top of the sail when the sub is sailing on the surface.

LEARN ABOUT:

Design of a Seawolf

Finding targets

Torpedoes

Two periscopes are in the center of the control room. One periscope is used in daylight. The other periscope is used in low-light conditions. This periscope has a TV camera. Pictures from the camera appear on TVs in the sub.

The control room also serves as an attack center. This room has several computers. Crew members use these computers to operate and aim weapons.

The control room is the center of operations for a submarine.

Living Space

A Seawolf submarine has a crew of 13 officers and 121 enlisted members. The living quarters are located in the sub's forward section. All crew members except the captain sleep in bunk beds. The captain has a private sleeping room.

Enlisted members eat their meals in the mess area. The mess area is the largest open area on a sub. It is located below the control room. Next to the mess area is the kitchen, or galley. Officers eat in a private dining area.

Sonar

A submarine crew cannot see underwater targets. The crew uses sonar to find targets.

Seawolf subs use two kinds of sonar. Active sonar locates underwater objects by bouncing sound waves off them. Passive sonar listens for sounds made by enemy submarines moving underwater.

Torpedo Room

The torpedo room holds racks of torpedoes and other weapons. Crews work together to load weapons into the torpedo tubes.

A Seawolf has eight torpedo tubes. These tubes are located on both sides of the hull. Both torpedoes and underwater mines are launched from the torpedo tubes.

Power Source

Seawolf subs are nuclear powered. The sub's nuclear reactor is located in the rear of the hull. It sends high-pressure steam to two turbine engines. These engines power the propeller. A Seawolf has a speed of about 28 miles (45 kilometers) per hour.

This painting is an artist's view of a Seawolf underwater.

The Seawolf Class

Function:	Attack submarine
Manufacturer:	General Dynamics Electric Boat Division
Date First Deployed:	1997
Length, overall:	353 feet (108 meters)
Width:	40 feet (12 meters)
Power Source:	One nuclear reactor, one propeller
Top Speed:	28 miles (45 kilometers) per hour
Maximum Diving Depth:	2,000 feet (610 meters)
Crew:	13 officers, 121 enlisted members

1 Hull

2 Sail

3 Propeller

4 Torpedo tube

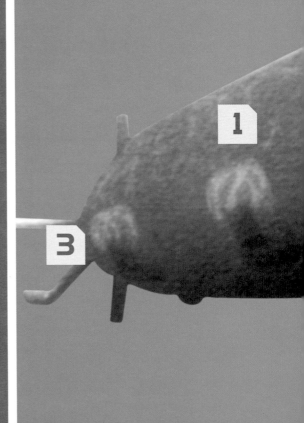

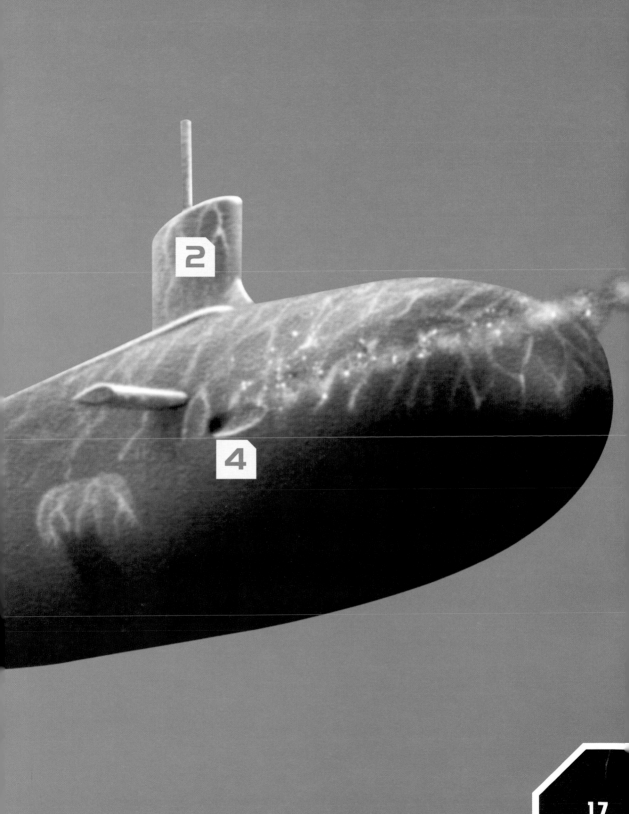

2

4

Tactics

The main job of a Seawolf submarine is to destroy enemy subs. It can also sink surface ships and launch missiles at land targets.

A Seawolf's crew uses the submarine's torpedo tubes to launch both torpedoes and missiles. Seawolf attack submarines carry MK-48 torpedoes and Tomahawk missiles.

Torpedoes

Each Seawolf is armed with antisubmarine torpedoes. These torpedoes are called MK-48s. They can be used against submarines and surface ships.

LEARN ABOUT:

Tomahawk missiles
Underwater mines
Locating enemies

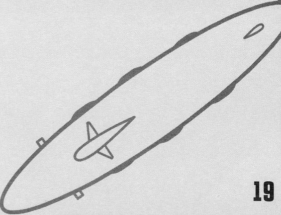

Crew members can track missiles launched from a Seawolf.

The MK-48 is designed to find and destroy enemy subs. Each MK-48 is equipped with sonar. The sonar guides the torpedoes directly to their target.

MK-48s can reach a sub moving at 35 miles (56 kilometers) per hour. Newer MK-48s can destroy subs traveling up to 46 miles (74 kilometers) per hour.

Cruise Missiles

Tomahawk cruise missiles are the Seawolf's other main weapon. The Seawolf carries Tactical Tomahawk missiles. These missiles are used against land targets.

When a Tactical Tomahawk launches from a Seawolf, a booster motor starts up. This motor propels the weapon out of the water and into the air. The booster motor then falls off, and a small engine starts. Small wings open from the sides of the missile. The small engine powers the missile to the land target.

The Tactical Tomahawk missile has a speed of about 550 miles (885 kilometers) per hour. A Global Positioning System (GPS) guides the weapon to the target.

U.S. Navy crews also can guide Tactical Tomahawk missiles in flight. These cruise missiles have a TV camera. When a target is not found, a weapons operator can change the missile's direction.

Mines

Seawolf subs carry several kinds of mines. An influence mine explodes when it senses a passing ship. Seawolf subs use a type of influence mine called the MK57 moored mine. These mines fasten themselves to the ocean floor.

A Seawolf also carries mobile mines. These mines sink to the ocean floor to wait for an enemy ship. These torpedo-powered mines then chase the enemy ship and hit it. Mobile mines can be programmed to chase only certain types of enemy subs.

Tomahawk cruise missiles are launched from attack subs.

The U.S. Navy's Seawolf subs search for enemy subs.

Finding Enemy Subs

A Seawolf has several ways to find enemy submarines. It can sail near an enemy's naval base. It waits for enemy subs to sail into open water and then attacks.

A Seawolf can also follow behind another U.S. Navy ship. The Seawolf then can destroy any enemy subs that follow the ship.

Seawolf crews depend on information from other Navy sources. These sources include Navy ships or spy satellites in space. Navy sources can alert a Seawolf to an enemy's location. Once a Seawolf receives this information, it can move quickly to the area. The Seawolf then uses its sonar to find the enemy sub. When the Seawolf's sonar finds the enemy, the crew will launch MK-48s. These powerful torpedoes will destroy the enemy sub.

CHAPTER 4

The Future

The Navy has three Seawolf class attack submarines. The USS *Jimmy Carter* is the newest attack submarine.

The USS *Jimmy Carter* has an extra 100-foot (30-meter) section added to the hull. This extra space will be a testing area. Crew members will test new equipment there, such as weapons and sensors.

New Attack Submarines

Today, the danger from Soviet subs is gone. But other countries have smaller subs. These subs may be a threat to the U.S. Navy during times of war.

LEARN ABOUT:

Third Seawolf sub

Virginia class

Equipment upgrades

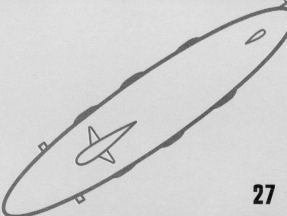

The Navy is preparing for this danger. It is building a smaller class of subs called the Virginia class.

Virginia class subs will have new features. The hull will have 12 missile launch tubes. A sub's crew will be able to fire multiple Tomahawk missiles in a single shot.

Another new feature will replace periscopes. The Virginia subs will use two imaging devices

The Virginia class is the Navy's new class of subs.

called photonics masts. These devices will send electronic images to screens in the control room. These devices will allow crew members to see objects outside the sub.

The newest class of attack submarines will not replace the Seawolf. Submarines in the Virginia class will operate mainly in shallow waters. The Navy's Seawolf class submarines will continue to patrol deeper water.

Glossary

Global Positioning System (GLOH-buhl puh-ZI-shuh-ning SISS-tuhm)—an electronic tool used to find the location of an object; this system is often called GPS.

mine (MINE)—an explosive device

missile (MISS-uhl)—an explosive weapon that can fly long distances

periscope (PER-uh-skope)—a tube-shaped viewing device

propeller (pruh-PEL-ur)—a set of rotating blades that provides thrust to move a ship through water

satellite (SAT-uh-lite)—a spacecraft that circles the earth; satellites gather and send information.

sensor (SEN-sur)—an instrument that detects physical changes in the environment

sonar (SOH-nar)—a device that uses sound waves to locate underwater objects

torpedo (tor-PEE-doh)—an explosive weapon that travels underwater

turbine engine (TUR-bine EN-juhn)—an engine powered by steam or gas; the steam or gas moves through the blades of a fanlike device and makes it turn.

Read More

Doyle, Kevin. *Submarines.* Military Hardware in Action. Minneapolis: Lerner, 2003.

Pascoe, Elaine, ed. *Seawolf Submarine.* Super Structures of the World. San Diego: Blackbirch Press, 2004.

Payan, Gregory. *Fast-attack Submarine: The Seawolf Class.* High-Tech Military Weapons. New York: Children's Press, 2000.

Internet Sites

FactHound offers a safe, fun way to find Internet sites related to this book. All of the sites on FactHound have been researched by our staff.

Here's how:

1. Visit *www.facthound.com*
2. Type in this special code **0736827218** for age-appropriate sites. Or enter a search word related to this book for a more general search.
3. Click on the **Fetch It** button.

FactHound will fetch the best sites for you!

Index